The Lynching of Sarah Elizabeth

The Lynching of Sarah Elizabeth
A CHOREOPOEM

© 2017 Ginger M Galloway. All rights reserved.
ISBN: 9780991297573

The Lynching of Sarah Elizabeth is a fictional account of the events surrounding the murder of Emmett Till. The characters and events depicted herein are the result of the imaginative creativity of the author. Any resemblance to any real people or events is absolutely coincidental. This is not a historical work and is intended to arouse the speculation of the reader about what could have happened.

Cover photo: https://www.flickr.com/photos/thepaperboy/2931192510

The Lynching of Sarah Elizabeth

A CHOREOPOEM BY

GINGER M. GALLOWAY

Table of Contents

SUMMARY ....*i*

CHARACTERS ....*iii*

ACT I

SCENE I *3*

    (prologue)

  EARL *3*

    The Abduction

SCENE II *9*

  MEN & WOMEN of MONEY, SARAH, STUCK *9*

    Money, Mississippi, 1965

SCENE III *15*

  SARAH *15*

    Life Work

  LES *16*

    Life Work

SARAH *20*

Blackberry Pie

SCENE IV *23*

　　　SARAH *23*

SCENE V *27*

　　　FOUR WOMEN *27*

SCENE VI *35*

　　　WHITE MAN *35*

The Interrogations

ACT II

SCENE I *41*

　　　SARAH *41*

The Prayer Vigil

　　　STUCK *45*

Stuck Speaks

SCENE II *47*

　　　EARL *47*

The Body

SCENE III *51*

    SARAH *51*

        This Is Wrong

    SARAH and LES *54*

        The Argument

    STUCK *58*

    SARAH *60*

        Sarah's Dream

    SARAH *62*

        Hanging

SCENE IV *67*

    WHITE MAN *67*

        The Burial

SCENE V *71*

    STUCK and LES *71*

        Sarah

SUMMARY

1965, Money, Mississippi. A young boy from Chicago Illinois goes to the deep south to visit his uncle for the summer. While there he is accused of "flirting" with the wife of a white shop owner. The boy is kidnapped from his uncle's home, beaten and murdered by a group of white men. Everyone in town knew it. There was certainly knowledge of the identity of the culprits and witnesses to the series of events. The case went to trial, nonetheless the men went free. Later those same men revealed the truth to the media free from Double Jeopardy. The men were never prosecuted for their crimes. The boy was Emmett Till.

But what if there were a woman? A simple woman who grew up in Mississippi and had lived through the vile atrocities of the south who had had enough and determined in her heart that what is right is right and what is wrong must be spoken of? What if she, against the urging of family and friends to keep her mouth shut because, *this is the south after all*, decided to speak up for the boy...to speak up for all of them?

This is the story of Sarah Elizabeth. She is that woman. But speaking up in Money, Mississippi--costs.

CHARACTERS

SARAH - 20-30 something African American woman determined that things must be different and that there must be change; somebody has to speak up against what is wrong in Money.

EARL - 40 something white male. Kidnapper and murderer. Full of hate.

LES - 30 something African American woman, older sister to Sarah. Angry about the situation in Money but hopeless and pessimistic about change.

STUCK - 20-30 something African American man, large stature. Stuck is what his name suggests: Stuck in his circumstance, willing to succumb to racism. Feels this is just the way things are.

WHITE MAN - 20's-40's white male. Elicits racism at its very worst.

MEN & WOMEN of MONEY - Various (10-15) African American men and women, all ages.

FOUR WOMEN - White women of Money. A cross section of the white community revealing racism mixed with just a hint of taboo.

ACT I

1965
Money, Mississippi
USA

ACT I
SCENE I
(prologue)

LES and SARAH'S house. One room shack on farmland. Small window over a pallet near the floor, stove, table, two chairs.

SARAH is asleep on the pallet. EARL creeps into the room.

EARL
The Abduction

We watched him leave out

He's a big blackey.
I'm sure there would have been casualties if we had to fight him.
Probably would have had to shoot him or cut him up real bad.
They don't like that.
No blood they say.
Not in the shack.

Bring her out they say.
She was sleep.
A wooden pallet near the floor.
A quilt. No pillow.

Her nightgown raised up on her thigh.
Thick dusty skin.

I don't mess with no darkies.
Nasty women
Lay with anything—
She was breathing out her mouth,
snoring soft.

I scared her
Pulling her to her feet
Her hair caught in my fingernails.

She smelled like sugar.
They all smell like sugar.
The canes marking her arms and legs
Deep white stripes
sealed with the sap—
Her hair thick but soft like a ram.

Her nails though were strong
slicing through the skin in my hand
But she didn't make a sound.
She knew I would be here tonight.
Baring her teeth down onto my forearm

I loosed her hair and punched her

Bright red blood dripping down her lips
Fat and round
She made no sound

That gown slipped up 'round her
as she fell backward on the cot.
I'd show her a lesson—

show her the place of a negro woman
I dropped down and held her there

Niggers ain't got sense
Still she didn't make a sound
Closed her eyes tight
She knew I would be here tonight.

Then I drug her body
Hands round her ankles.
That gown slipped clean over her head.
I drug her all the way into the field
Where the brothers waited
Johnson called out—
He thinks I'm stupid or something
But he don't know I kill a white man too
Tells me I'm dragging that nigger
cutting stones into her back
a trail of blood shining behind her
in the moonlight

She didn't make a sound
Twisting and turning her body
Hands grabbing at the earth
She spit on my back—

Warm saliva between my shoulder blades
causing my shirt to stick there
I dropped her feet and kicked her

I kicked that negro woman so hard in
her breast
she called out then

A loud scream, that fades, then quiet

but Jesus can't hear niggers
calling his name in vain

Somebody tossed me the rope then.
I suppose they wasn't man enough to
fight her
or strong enough to rinse her blood
from their hands—
Hooded fools

As I knelt down to cinch the noose
she bit me again
on my left arm, just above the elbow.
I smacked her with the back of my
hand
her tooth stuck in my wrist—
I heard them slap the horse.

Her body rose up out of my hands
Warm piss raining down on me
as that niggers feet kicked the air
above my head

She didn't make a sound.

End Scene I

ACT I
SCENE II

A busy small-town street. Businesses including Bryant's storefront. Men and women walk around and alternately voice lines or grouping of lines.

MEN & WOMEN of MONEY, SARAH, STUCK
(voiced together/several actors - alternately)
Money, Mississippi, 1965

Normalcy
Saturday night jukebox
Big city takin'
it's time

Movin' slow like the south

Southern
Finger snappin'
Hip shakin'
Pressed up against hot bodies
Party's happenin'
Everything's copastetic

Full of liquor

Fresh conked hair of the boys up from

Jackson

Jive talkin'

Buicks an' hogs lined up
Engines roarin'

Press n' curls bouncing off
can curlers
Girls leaning against fenders
White socks and petticoats
Home by ten
Boys trying to cop a feel
The night giving way to

Boys driving south

or north

to the city

Avoiding
Sunday morning
Church bells ringing
awake

Hung over coffee black

Rhythmic thumping and clapping of
hands
The windows are open
White inside and out

Even Jesus
Looking at negroes singin'

Gospel hymns
Walls jumping
Holy Ghost and paper fans
Blowing around in thick Mississippi air

Kitchens where chicken will fry tonight
Hot grease popping

Greens simmering in great black pots

Soft peas and rice

Sweet tea and honey'd lemon

On the porch
Guitar strummin'

Swattin' at mosquitoes and catchin'
Fire flies

The night will be short

    STUCK puts his arm around SARAH

SARAH
    Big arms wrapping around

STUCK
> Soft skin
> oils and jasmine
> Lavender scent rising

SARAH
> Claiming he is mine

> > *STUCK teases SARAH*
> Too hot for foolishness

STUCK
> Southern hot

Damp sheets
To keep cool

Work comes before the sun

Strong backs
Pullin' and pickin'

And totin'

Back and forth

Pink babies callin' on negro women
Feed 'em
Walkin' at night

Arms wide
Waitin'

Funny place
The south

Still in the past

Reachin' for tomorrow's
Normal

End Scene II

ACT I
SCENE III

Inside and outside SARAH and LES' house. SARAH is cooking dinner inside, LES peeling potatoes outside.

SARAH
Life Work

Life be work, work in the morning
work at bed, all that work in between

even making love is
work, all that
sweating and hopping but it do
to laugh and I got me a man
and Les stay mad at me and I can't
figure
Why she don't think this girl ain't a
child.

Life be good, blackberries be sweet
and oh when Stuck kisses me,

and sometimes the white folk don't
mind

can't she see that, my own sister
just as mad and busting out the seams
'cause I'm smiling
and I'm proud.

Life be soft, like that spot
under the arm, like this clean skin
washing, wash
a dress 'til it be good
as new and rock
a body to dream like the way I feel
down inside when that man look at me

all these folks eating up they sad
afraid to stomp and speak and laugh

Life be me, singing this silly song
and good and proud, I'm gonna stay
proud
no matter what foolishness Les say
I ain't afraid, and I can
dance and twirl around
and set my hair, and love me
somethin', and make a pie
today, and go be
with my he.

LES
Life Work

Life be hard
I remember dusty sweat coating my
lips
and dripping into my eyes.
Wiping my face and looking across the
field.

Mississippi sunshine bouncing
Dancing through the tall grass
Dark silhouettes bent on the horizon.
Faint bellow of hymn stoked cane stalks
Knife slid into sheath
Tooled leather, hand stitched.
Rows of cane infatuated.
Hushed whispers.
Mother.
Sarah's mother's voice.
Echoed soft and gentle.
Only in the dark
Only at night.
I couldn't see her in the shadows of the sun.
Hidden in daylight.
I looked across the field
The workers could have been her brothers, or cousins, or uncles
I didn't know
Sarah didn't ask who they were
She wanted to know whose she was
Belonging to me wasn't enough
It had never been enough
I knew it never would.
Her dark skin repeating generations
Thick complexion like motor grease dripping
The voice like bullfrog song
The inside of hands brown
The bottom of feet
Fatherless children, had been easy to

release
His spirit had been caught up in the night
Long white stains on his cheeks
The pain had woke him
Held him and wouldn't let him call out
I found him
Stiff
Cold
White stains on his cheeks
I cleaned his face before I called the undertaker.
Sarah asked seven times.
Once each year after he died
Until her thirteenth birthday
So she could save him in her mind
No more asking.
She finally allowed him to leave her like mother left me
Gently on butterflies wings
Mama's voice
Silent
No one to tell the story
Reveal the secret
Smear with lies.
Looking out across the field
A small wooden faced house
Painted white
Built by father's hands
His hands, my hands
And Sarah's
Girls need their mother

to teach them
who they are
Where they belong
Sharing the differences
likenesses
of daughters
                Les wipes her face

sliding the knife into it's place
Life is hard working in a barren
field

SARAH is doing housework, making the bed, preparing to bake, finds containers empty.

SARAH
Blackberry Pie

Purple balls growing
out behind Jones' field waiting to be
pressed to blackberry pie.

Thought Les was my mama
til I was four and Grandma
pointed out a tall lady
stooped over in the fields.

Grandma said that tall lady was my mama
and it was she, not Les who curled
round me made sure I had clothes,
made sure I was behaved, made sure I
had my beans.

Oooh that day I screamed, made Les so
mad she wouldn't talk to me and ooooh
I had to see.

So that night I stayed up, our shack,
cold and blank, the stars above us
old bent men winking their wings. I
waited and waited, watching for mama,
thin she'd be, ghost or haint

strange, a tall dark lady with long
soft hands, someone who never scream
or whoop me.

She'd touch my hair and whisper my
name. She'd settle besides my frame,
her sweat like wine, my fingers
curled around her hair.

But no one came, no one but my
sister-mama, snoring hard better dare
not wake.

A pie, maybe something sweet, Les
could eat two slices, we need a pie,
a change from the taste of salt and
rice and beans.

End Scene III

ACT I
SCENE IV

*SARAH walking toward Bryant's store.
She has a bag for groceries.*

SARAH

It's August hot and fierce
with this dust
kicking up and those boys
laughing
so loud.

Stuck would rip into
them something
fierce tell them its too hot
to be out here
Fussing and cussing and acting
fool but they sure is having fun.

Young boys laughing, still dressed
for the field, denim and dirt
open mouths

How they skinny knees
ever turn to a man.

Like my man, Stuck
big and strong, gentle, quiet
as a cloud
With his black eyes
Just for me.

*Stops at the door and looks toward
the store.*

That's Simon. And Bobo
from Chicago. Too big to be
a boy. Too big and
don't he walk
like he free..

If only me and Stuck
can go to Chicago.
We'd dance
and sing. Must be heaven
to go to a place
where they teach you '
to hold your back straight.
spend all
Day making love dancing
On the street.

Instead of Money, a town
Of broke things. People
Struggling just dream. Money
Like the sound of it
Would make up for the lack
Like the name is enough.

Nah, Chicago sounds like a song
Got a bite to it, place must
Blackberry sweet.

End Scene IV

ACT I
SCENE V

FOUR WOMEN on a bench in front of Bryant's store. The American Flag is on a post above their heads.

FOUR WOMEN

UNISON

    The American Flag

WOMAN 1
    Whipping the air outside the doorpost

WOMAN 2
    Flap slap flap
    A syncopation that breaks the monotony

WOMAN 3
    Keeps out the flies

WOMAN 4
    Southern
    August is hot

WOMAN 4
    Mississippi heat
    Damp
    Sultry

WOMAN 2
    Handkerchief in apron pocket
    Dabbing wet makeup -- balmy skin

WOMAN 3
    June Bug
    Blue iridescence
    hypnotized by the gold lancet
    Tangled, twisting in the flag
    Flung against the jam

WOMAN 1
    Hideous buzz

WOMAN 2
    Shop

WOMAN 3
    Sheets of golden sun slipping away

  Sundries and meat
  Credit

WOMAN 1
  No Whites only
  No Negroes only
  No bathroom
  No shoes, no shirt

WOMAN 3
  Sentry

WOMAN 2
  Jingle, jangle
  Announcer
  Pronounced
  All entrance and egress

WOMAN 3
  One

WOMAN 4
  He came in with his eyes on me
  I never seen eyes like that
  Never
  Not on a human or an animal
  He don't look like them
  Bright skin

WOMAN 1
    And his hair's not nappy

WOMAN 4
    Loose
    He smiled
    Straight white teeth

WOMAN 3
    He's not from here

WOMAN 4
    New denim
    Not the worn overalls of the local boys
    The same color as
    His eyes
    Still planted
    Still asking questions that his teeth won't   release
    Finally asking for sweet
    Absent the thick drawl
    The tell-tale evidence
    of southern existence
    Reflective, like marbles
    Those eyes don't bounce from

     counter to floor
     Stayed on me
     Until placing his change
     White counter
     Three copper coins
     He caught them in his cupped hand
     Brushing against mine
     Heart beating in my throat I pulled my hand   back

WOMAN 1
     I've never been touched

WOMAN 3
     Looked at

WOMAN 2
     With eyes on a negro that looked
     like they belong on a white man

WOMAN 4
     Blood rushing to my face
     as panic settled on my skin
     What if Juanita had seen
     Could see
     Willing my cheeks to drain
     I touched the place where our hands had   touched

        What if he knew
        If he could tell
        The evidence hidden in my heartbeat
        and in those eyes

WOMAN 1
        Outside
        In a circle
        Standing drop-hipped

WOMAN 2
        Talking loud

WOMAN 3
        Slapping hands
        Laughter

WOMAN 4
        Dark skinned
        Ashy knuckles
        Waving at June Bug
        Freed

WOMAN 2
        Glistening reflection
        Glass sparkles

WOMAN 3
    Wind chimes
    Dancing

WOMAN 4
    Gold Ring

WOMAN 1
    Thin finger
    Red polish

WOMAN 2
    Handkerchief dabbing

WOMAN 3
    waving

WOMAN 1
    The American Flag
    Reminder

WOMAN 2
    Whipping the air outside the doorpost

End Scene V

ACT I
SCENE VI

WHITE MAN in the street in front of the store. African American's of Money walking back and forth on the street.

WHITE MAN
The Interrogations

The shoes of dead men don't pace floors
But what we got here is comfortable leather
Hard soles
The feet of a negro walking
Short steps watching their own feet
Like to know where they go.

You the one?
Noisy soles, ticky-tap?
Or maybe it's you?
Quick speech and sass on your tongue.
You look suspicious
Your mouth turned down
Dumb don't speak
Too simple to be the one
Was you at the market today?
A lyin' nigger's good as dead
Dead don't climb no stair
Was it you?

Grab her hand
Pull her close
Whisper in her ear?
Was it you?
Defile the woman
With your nasty disease?
Don't you know your place, boy?
Was it you?
Skin like butterfat
Hair like wool
Eyes like glass
You know him don't you?
You know who he is.
We gonna find us a negro
We gonna find him
And make sure he don't pace no more.

End of Scene VI

END OF ACT I

ACT II

ACT II
SCENE I

The scene is a well-to-do home. Bedroom, living room and kitchen are visible. There is a bed, couch, and table. STUCK, and SARAH, are surrounded by others

SARAH
The Prayer Vigil

Stuck and I walked in
The room was full and thick
The call had gone
The neighbors had come
Stockinged feet
They were all there
Junebug and his sister
the girl with the limp
Elder Jenkins and Sister Rose
Betty Ann and her boys;
Tiny and Big Arm
Sula and Sissy-- the twins
Red had her hair tied in a silk scarf
Crimson pin curls peeking out at her temple
They were all there
Pastor laying hands
like he wasn't the one needing prayer
Stuck looking at me

Me looking at him
The night air, hot and humid
pushing the curtains back and forth
in the room
We grew up in Mississippi
Coexisting in an uncomfortable way
Our eyes spoke with glued lips
Things we dared not say on the walk
down the road
Dared not say it in this crowded room
Elder Parks and his sickly wife
Mister Donnie Marks
Deacon was there in a fine blue coat
They held hands
Holding on like by pure will they
could bring him back
Like he would walk out of the
darkness
Onto the porch of the preacher's
house
He would smile at them
Eyes closed I pretended to be
listening
praying the prayer
echoing the long "mmhmm's" and "yes,
Lord's"
Oil slick and dripping
Windows sweating from the breath
Too many people in the small house.
Beds with sheets turned down
Everyone standing around
Housecoats and sweaters draped over
nightgowns

Men who had taken the time to throw on pants and boots
It was late and people started to yawn
They were all there
One big family rallied around
the vigil for the boy from out of town
Eight days ago he was a stranger
Talking funny and snapping chewing gum
Tonight
The neighbors stood elbow to elbow
Everyone pretending reality didn't exist
Someone fanning the preacher's wife
A white lace fan unfurled from the end table
"Sarah, you pray now."
Full of tears overflowing I stopped looking at the door
I stopped looking for fancy shoes
I stopped expecting to see him walk through
As if this were a dream
Women humming the hymn
Bodies rocking
I forced the words into the room
Heavenly Father slipping through my lips
What could I tell him that he didn't already know
That they hadn't told?

What could I ask?
When God decided to let them take him
Didn't He decide they would send him back
Harmless boy child
A big child without sense enough to keep his mouth shut
A smart aleck boy
Who would mouth off and talk back
Forgot who his people were
That in the south we don't act like we don't know
So I asked Jesus to close his mouth that those bastards might show him mercy
And I would have believed it myself
If I wasn't from the south
Mississippi
from Money
Where a white man and his white wife ran the only sundry in town
Making their living off poor black folks
who don't act like segregation ended and they didn't get word that things' diff'rent
But they were all there
Every one
In Jesus' name
I said as the men started to move toward the door
Flashlights in hand
Enough time

They had gauged
It was time to bring him home
Tell him about the south
Tell him about being a negro
Tell him
Before they kill him
Amen

    spotlight zooms down on STUCK

STUCK
Stuck Speaks

Should have taught that boy
better, should have schooled
him proper on how to bow
down fetch, look at a woman
without looking, should have
told him this world could end
at the end of a rope off of
one misstep, should have
beat him, tied him down
choked his neck til that smile
and whistle shut up, should
have told him that he
ain't nothing but a
mule, and a dangerous one
at that, liable to kick when
the chain is too tight, liable
to bite, should have grabbed
that boy and shook him
til the only thing on him
worth being seen, the white

teeth, the smile, fell out
and his big city shoulders
slumped
over like mine

                        End Scene I

ACT II
SCENE II

At night in front of the store, EARL is talking (to himself) while other white men are gathered and appear to be giving and receiving a report of the nights events

EARL
The Body

Darkness covering
Charcoal skies
Only the headlights shone
Thin beacons of light
Dust rising from the tires
Riding
Three up front
Three in back
Summer air moist to the skin
A cool breeze before the sun's face
Sunlight slowly meeting with the horizon
Following
Revealing
Shading night-time eyes with bloody palms
Pulling into town at day break
Gravel crackling under the tires
Goodyear
Maybe
Burlap tarp

Pulled over dusty shoes
Socks
No point in socks
Told there was no point in socks
Ridiculous
Dust dancing as the truck lurched forward
Bundle sliding
Work boots kicking back
Sliding into place
Brown leather
like leopard coats
Spotted
Jumping from the bed
Displacing
Menacing
Clouds of dust shooting out
As if
Secrets told
Low voices
Rumbling the report
Shimmery whispers
Bitter breath
Urine
Beer
Swamp water
Too early for people
Way to early
Sashay
As if early were late
The early sun disconnected
Eyes connected and torn
Crossing

Wide
Eyes tight
Sideways
"Load up!"
Boots kicking off the sideboard
Fresh mark
Wet
Caught in the web
Of the burlap

End Scene II

ACT II
SCENE III

SARAH, LES and STUCK in Sarah and Les' cottage. *SARAH is pacing. LES and STUCK are seated at the table.*

SARAH
This Is Wrong

This is wrong
say God spanks a body
Hits with his big hand the gristle
The thick flesh
Say God has even the angels
Spit and cast eyes on the sin
Even then it would be softer
Than a truck full of white
Men and the town listening
To a boy being beat

Say a punishment was earned
That the bad thought was kept with
Sugar teeth, that the thief was not hesitating
To eat, say even if being sorry
Was forgot
The punishment don't fit the crime
and
I can't find the reason in this

Did he touch that white girl
or tear through

Her linen.

A patch of rags lined
The sound of slaps
Rage and thud-like dark leaned
Over into the thick of my
Breast as if I sat with him in the
front seat He don't even come from
here.

How can we stand it the watching
The praying and waiting
Of it, teeth in our mouths like
Crooked rocks
they kill him
And we watch and nod and sing

I done asked God to bring him home
It's not enough to sit and wait

Somewhere there might be a path
In front, lined with soldiers or
Winged girls, the fabric billowing
out
The cotton turn to shiny dust
Like fresh sheets or berries
like the leaves of mint
A wind cool and supple
pushing past our lips

Somewhere there is worth
A man is more than his skin, his
fault or

desire nothing but infant steps
the innocent reaching out like
Fingers to flame
sweet curiosity

How can we walk the good road knowing
That in the car he sat quiet, so scared
Staring back at the black faces
That didn't wall themselves
Around him, that didn't help
but pointed him out
hid behind hands
slunk like cowards away

How can we think of children, babies
Our mothers knowing that there
is a tall big boned boy, a child, a flower
An insect covered in rain bowing out its
Long legs, grass and sunlight
Breath and bone being
Crushed by a weight
It should not bear

This is wrong

And the cords that bind
Us to each other, the human and the life
Snapping like branches with this loss
Of protection

>   Or witness will snap back at us
>
>   he is of us
>   he is us
>   We let him go
>   We pushed him in
>   The hole, the truck, the riverbed
>   We whooped him quiet,
>   We ignored him cold

SARAH and LES
The Argument

LES
No matter
Death gone come
Blood boiling for the boy
But it come
By hand or by Heaven

>   SARAH
>   Death has his turn.
>   Time pushing against itself.
>   Somebody got to speak
>   Raise their voice and say it
>   Darkness ain't light
>   Flowers that never bloom
>   Birds that never sing
>   The world just mixed up
>   It ain't right

LES
Thoughts about what's right
When right don't matter
Right ain't real
What's right is a lie
You delighting in lies
Dreams of what ain't ever gon' be made
Right

                                              SARAH
        Tomorrow can be what today ain't
        Dreams transformed into a reality
                Winds lifting up and
                Changing direction
                    Moving things

LES
Hurricanes are wind
Moving every which-a-way
Destruction in their path
Moving things that weren't meant to be
Moved
You like the winds
Lifting up trash

                                              SARAH
                You just lost your hope
          Tomorrows stuck in yesterdays
              Things ever the same
              Stagnant and stale

                    No dividing lines between
                 Living this life and the next
                                         Angry
                                      Dejected
                                      Drowning
        Life can't change cause you won't let
                                            it

LES
Dredging flour on fish that turned
Pretending that rotting flesh ain't
Rotten

                                         SARAH
                                    Pretending
                                Dead fish swim
                    Your lie is bigger than mine
            Acting like the future is promised
                                       It ain't
                          So we raise our voices
            Screams from the depth of souls lost

LES
Raising voices in the dark
Emptiness that no one can hear
through
No one tries to look through

                                         SARAH
                                         Alone
                                   In the dark
                         I will make a sound

                    A sound that breaks rocks
            And causes clouds to give up on
                                    raindrops

LES
Waiting on buzzards
Lying on cold earth
Above the place where they will break
the ground
Pine box lowered by droop-eyed men
Tired
Burying they own
Children
Without futures
Because futures are dreams
Broken with the first rays of
tomorrow

                                        SARAH
                    Tomorrow has promise
            No matter if anyone believes
                                    She comes
        She pours herself into time and space
                                    Dependent
            On the movement of men and women
                            Who dare to move

LES
Lost days
Lost lives
The cost that all of us will pay

                             SARAH
                   Whatever it cost.

      LES leaves the room. STUCK speaks.

                   STUCK

      Hush
      Night stretches over us like big arms
      Pillows our head
      Invisibility a blackness behind
      Black and yes baby
      you hush
      lay down here
      fall into that space
      Wlll here everything is drifting on
      each small touch

      Know what I see, you and me
      And that constant laughing sound
      You make, so happy with little things
      A flower in your hair, a bright color
      A good dream
                         Strokes her hair.

      What more can we do but wait,
      pray
      Night is a coat stuffed with down
      Night is medication for pain
      warm milk to cover us to go to dream

This be over soon

Think of morning, the way heaven's gates
Will hold us

What would you have us do

This anger don't become you, you should be
Humming, hushing a baby, hushing yourself
Laying in my arms and in my smile
bright and sweet curled like a leaf
In my palm

Remember how I got my name?
Four years old
And hands too big.
Got my hand stuck in that jelly jar.
Couldn't wait for the biscuits
Had to have it now.
A whole day hand stuck in the jar
Til' Mama came home

A woman ain't a man 'cause
She got patience
Her fight is to wait
Be patient and hold on

Sarah climbs into bed, turns her back to Stuck

I got to keep you safe, Sarah,
we got to keep us safe and this
This is the sacrifice we make

It wasn't me in that truck
And you raise up like he your man
Or your baby

Foolish boy reaching in the jelly jar

Sarah it wasn't me, and I promise you
It will never be
                      STUCK leaves.

SARAH
              Looks to see him leave.

But it ain't right, Stuck, none of
it.   This is wrong.

Spotlight centers on SARAH in bed.
She tosses in fitful sleep.

SARAH
Sarah's Dream

They used to tease me about my skin
Black and pock marked
Until I would cry and run away

Grandma's house was down the road
She would meet me at the door
tears running down my face

She never reprimanded them
It was part of growing up she would say
Part of becoming who you are

Her dark hands would wipe
lines of water from my cheeks
and her lips would pop against my forehead

She wouldn't pacify me
Just set me in the big chair
A bowl of peas that need shucking

Before dark she would make me a sandwich
Potted meat, bread from her oven
And send me home

I would walk back slow
kicking dirt and rocks
Never settled in my soul

Lights dim, SARAH lays down.
EARL enters the room.

SARAH
Hanging

Somebody got to speak out
Somebody got to say what needs to be said
When I allow poison words roll
From these lips
Arms are bared
The worst creeps to the surface
And the stench of death overcomes
But somebody got to say
And that's why I knew
That's why when the wind kicked in
Through the open door
I didn't pull the cover
Like meeting death where he works
Expectation
Stuck couldn't protect us now
Somebody would stand and
Somebody would die
Gagging on
Breath like rancid meat
Body hairy and stench like a mule
Determined this wasn't the time for words
Lips tied
Hands free
Lifted like a rag doll
Swinging like a wild dog
Silent
Daddy taught me silence
Weapon more deadly than sound

Slicing and ripping and biting
In silence
The sting of locked fist
My breath caught and arrested
The taste of my own blood
Pressing thin lips over broken teeth
Hard against mine
Hot tongue
Breath
Sightless
Knees and elbows
Arms
Legs twisted
Wrenching exposed loins
Blood for blood
A cloud of foul air
Moving and spinning around
"A Woman's place"
Echoing in my ear
I don't have no place
Brown leather boot finding a space
Between ribs
Air
Forcing slits of eyes to watch
The sole rise
Dropping solid
Air
Flaccid arms
Useless
Every muscle forcing lips to remain
Silent
Air
Slid across wooden slat

Head bouncing
from the step
Somebody got to say, Les
Somebody got to say
Air
Stones digging
All the fight in the will
Not to die on this road
Not to die pleading
Air
Words that matter
Only those
Because I understand
Wisdom in silence
Strength in speaking
Air
'Cause somebody got to say
Somethin'
I knew they was comin'
Determined
Now
Silent

End Scene III

ACT II
SCENE IV

Night, outside in the wood, a large patch of dirt. WHITE MAN is burying something.

WHITE MAN
The Burial

Like a dog, man loves to dig, dig
earth through the fingers, brown
dirt on white knuckles,
feels good the way
even a nigga's color falls
Cool dirt on hot skin
Cause it do make the blood
Hot this work or cleansing

We was meant to dig and throw clumps
in the hole, cover a black
thigh, a foot, dig and throw more
dirt, until
the clearing is stable
Til all the world know
That there are places for people
Places of standing for men
Places of sitting for boy
Places up high for women
Places down low for whores
And places like this
For those that refuse to fit in

He stands and sighs

Shovel to gun to shoulder to throat
to sky, to earth a cleansing is a
burial
A way of putting it back
In perspective
Some men kill
And forget that cleaning
Is the best part, the covering
And making right of the sin

Feels good to dig and cover
Pat and shovel. This here patch
Is my own little girl safe
From black eyes and muscles,
And this here clump is the wife
Who won't dare be seduced
By darkie breath, and here
Right here is the end of the way
That black woman
Seduces me.

That final scream, see the red
under the black, perhaps if that
thing
Under this dirt is stomped out
Then I can go home
And enjoy the cornmeal
The beef and cake, without
Thinking of my own daddy's belt
And my own mama's cold hate.

This is cleansing dirt, keeps me
Clean, dig and turn
dirt in my pores like a souvenir

End Scene IV

ACT II
SCENE V

Stage is black, no setting. STUCK and LES enter each from stage right and left.

STUCK and LES
Sarah

STUCK
Sarah

                                      LES
                            Sister Sarah

STUCK
Sweet Sarah
Sharing breath
and heartbeat
Dancing together
No music
to catch our steps
Just the rhythm of lovers

                                      LES
             Drawn out of who you are
                     Becoming who
       Living a life of confusion
                      Your destiny

                    tossed by the side of the road
                          Dust kicking up in summer
                                                Heat

STUCK
Sarah
Strong Sarah
Standing beneath
lifting me up
Into royalty
Coming from nowhere
Going nowhere
She sees me
Just the rhythm of lovers

                                               LES
                                      Sister Sarah
                          Who you are is skipping
                                      Life moving
                           in rainbow colors and
                                  puppies breath
                             Stagnant in summer
                                             Heat

STUCK
Sarah
Sweet Sarah
Singing and crying
her emotions tied
to the lives of others
Moving her heart
To match
Sympathy as she marks time

Makes me love her
Just the rhythm of lovers

                              LES
                     Sister Sarah
                 You still a negro
                    You still one
               Moving through today
                as if you were not
              Dancing in this world
                         Despised
                           Sister
             Strangled by the South
                  Southern living
                Money, Mississippi
                             Heat

The Lynching of Sarah Elizabeth

A CHOREOPOEM BY
GINGER M. GALLOWAY

Ginger M. GALLOWAY Poet, playwright, author, and artist. Her published works include "Destiny Interrupted" (2013), her self-illustrated picture storybook "What I Really Want to Be" (2012), and three collections of poetry;  *Beans - A small book of poetry for young children* (2001), *Skipping Rope* (2013), and *Cacao and Coffee Beans* (2013). Ginger has written and produced the stage plays *I Just Wanna Be Me* (2012), *Good Ain't Good Enough* (2014) and *Illusions* (2014).

Ginger is a freelance writer and graphic artist in Southern California where she lives with her husband and four of their seven children.

gingermgalloway@gmail.com
mommygalloway.blogspot.com

Also find Ginger M. Galloway on Facebook and Amazon.

www.ingramcontent.com/pod-product-compliance
Lightning Source LLC
Chambersburg PA
CBHW020949090426
42736CB00010B/1330